BE A LLAMA

& stay a little calmer

BE A LLAMA
& stay a little calmer

SARAH FORD

ILLUSTRATED BY
ANITA MANGAN

spruce

NOTES

Read this book before going to bed for a better night's sleep.

Contains a literary chill pill – no other medication necessary.

No rating, it's all cool, man.

Not for the hurrying kind.

Spread the calm.

Be like Llama. Why? Because she is friendly, good-natured, peace-lloving and calm. Llama does not llet llife get her down – she just lloves every minute of it.

Llama trots through llife gently – the only thing that weighs her down is her hair. She lloves to show her individuality and quirkiness with her many styles. She is chilled with a capital C, never happier than when she's socializing with her herd... friendly and charming, she's always got your back. Don't be fooled by her eyelashes – she is surprisingly smart, and if you push her too far, she'll warn you off with a llittle spit, especially if you try to graze on her patch.

Llama will enrich your llife with her grace and charm, and her natural curiosity is contagious. She is just as happy humming a llittle tune by herself, or staying at home in her jjamas, as she is on a big night out with the girls. It's all good when you're with Llama. Llive your llife llike Llama and there will be no drama.

**LLAMA'S
10 RULES FOR
A GOOD LIFE**

- Don't sweat the small stuff – no one likes a sweaty llama. If you worry about things and they do go wrong then it's doubly bad.

- Keep it real, feet firmly planted on the floor – no drama, Llama.

- Slow down, it's not a race.

- Stop thinking, clear your brain, have a little rest and a cup of tea, little cracker and a little bit of cheese.

- Wear your lucky pants – what could possibly go wrong with those bad boys on board?

- Realize that you are just a dot on the landscape. If you don't make a deadline, the world will still go round, it's not the end of the world.

- To release a bit of stress, challenge your chum to a game of thumb war (temporarily forget you are a llama as it's a bit difficult to do with hoofies).

- Don't be scared, try new things, rise to the challenge – and when you have a go, you will feel invincible.

- Enjoy the journey, the rough and the smooth... the road might be long but it's all amazing.

- Sometimes you just have to say no. If you take on too much, then you will burn out and lose your calm, so get to know your limits.

Llama was not going to make a mountain out of a molehill.

Llama thought you had to experience pain in order to know happiness.

Llama was imagining
that everyone in the
audience was on the loo.

Llama felt very small.

Llama had let her
hair down.

Llama was spending
all day in her jjamas.

Llama had lowered
the bar.

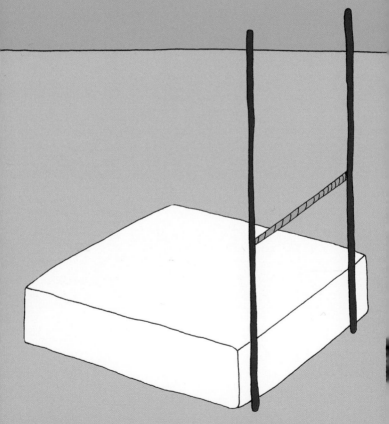

Talking to old
people at bus stops
was Llama's thing.

Llama expected her husband to leave his undies on the floor.

It was the end of a tough day and Llama had loosened the elastic.

Llama was at peace when knitting.

Llama asked herself
whether it would
really matter in five
years' time.

Llama was looking
at things from a
different angle.

Llama asked herself
whether she really
needed them.

Llama tried to concentrate on her breathing but her nose hairs were tickling.

Llama just said
'Uhh, ohh.'

Llama waited for
the storm to pass.

Llama was sorting out her sock drawer.

Llama had gone
for a long walk.

Llama was looking at
old family photos.

Llama had heard that kiwi fruit aided sleep.

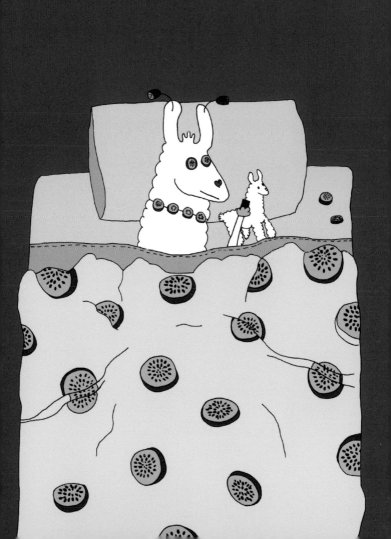

Llama had cut out
the caffeine.

Llama was visualizing her island of peace.

Kneading dough got rid of all Llama's frustration.

The cat pose was Llama's
favourite yoga position.

Llama was breathing in
the scented garden.

Having all her ducks in a row helped Llama to make sense of things.

Llama found her
lavender pillow
a bit spiky.

Resting her amethyst crystal on her forehead was more difficult than Llama had thought.

Llama was squeezing
her stress ball.

Reciting her favourite limerick made Llama crack up. 'There was an old llama from Palma...'

Llama felt that the power of hugging should not be underestimated.

Llama had got up before everyone else.

Llama had carried
out a random act of
kindness.

Llama wasn't sure if chicken soup was good for her soul, but it did taste yummy.

Llama had honey on
her mind and bees
chasing her.

Reggae Llama didn't worry about a thing.

Doing the dishes slowly
softened Llama's hoofies
and her handies.

Llama decided to
go fly a kite.

Llama thought that
bouncing on her bed
was the best kind
of therapy.

Llama liked helping the chicken to cross the road.

Inhaling Llama,

exhaling Llama

Sleeping under the stars was Llama's favourite thing ever.

Now take a chill pill
and be a llama.

An Hachette UK Company
www.hachette.co.uk

First published in Great Britain in
2018 by Spruce, an imprint of
Octopus Publishing Group Ltd
Carmelite House
50 Victoria Embankment
London EC4Y 0DZ
www.octopusbooks.co.uk

Distributed in the US by
Hachette Book Group
1290 Avenue of the Americas
4th and 5th Floors
New York, NY 10104

Distributed in Canada by
Canadian Manda Group
664 Annette St.
Toronto, Ontario, Canada M6S 2C8

ISBN 978-1-84601-562-5

A CIP catalogue record for this
book is available from the British
Library.

Printed and bound in Europe

10 9 8 7 6 5 4 3

Commissioning Editor
Sarah Ford

Assistant Editor
Ellie Corbett

Designer and Illustrator
Anita Mangan

Senior Designer
Jaz Bahra

Production Controller
Sarah Kulasek-Boyd